P9-CQV-622

The Science of Living Things

What is a Marsupial?

Bobbie Kalman & Heather Levigne

Crabtree Publishing Company

The Science of Living Things Series
A Bobbie Kalman Book

**To Sandy Rowden,
with thanks for her love and support**

Editor-in-Chief
Bobbie Kalman

Writing Team
Bobbie Kalman
Heather Levigne

Managing Editor
Lynda Hale

Editor
Hannelore Sotzek

Copy Editor
John Crossingham

Computer Design
Lynda Hale

Production Coordinator
Hannelore Sotzek

Photo Researcher
Heather Levigne

Special thanks to
Wendy Crossingham

Consultant
Debbi McCollum, M. Ed.,
Education Curator, The Montgomery Zoo, Alabama

Photographs
Animals Animals: Phyllis Greenberg: page 4
Erwin and Peggy Bauer: title page, pages 10, 13, 20 (top), 21
Libby Crossingham: page 31 (bottom)
C. Andrew Henley/Larus: front cover, pages 5, 8, 9 (top), 11,
    14, 15 (top), 17, 18, 19, 24, 25 (both)
Tom Stack & Associates: Mark Newman: page 30; Inga Spence: page 16;
    Dave Watts: pages 12-13, 15 (bottom), 20 (bottom), 22, 23, 26, 27, 28
Other images by Digital Stock

Illustrations
All illustrations by Barbara Bedell

Digital Prepress
Embassy Graphics

Printer
Worzalla Publishing Company

Crabtree Publishing Company

PMB 16A
350 Fifth Ave.,
Suite 3308
New York, NY
10118

612 Welland Ave.
St. Catharines,
Ontario,
Canada
L2M 5V6

73 Lime Walk
Headington,
Oxford
OX3 7AD
United Kingdom

Cataloging in Publication Data
Kalman, Bobbie
    What is a marsupial?

(The science of living things)
Includes index.

ISBN 0-86505-978-0 (library bound) ISBN 0-86505-955-1 (pbk.)
This book describes the physical characteristics, behavior, and habitat
of the main types of marsupials and the differences between them and
placental mammals, including reproduction, gestation, and birth.

1. Marsupials—Juvenile literature. [1. Marsupials.] I. Levigne, Heather.
II. Title. III. Series: Kalman, Bobbie. Science of living things.

QL737.M3 L48 2000   j599.2   LC 99-085748
                                                    CIP

Contents

What is a marsupial?

Marsupials are **mammals**. Mammals are **warm-blooded**—their body can adjust so that its temperature stays the same in hot or cold surroundings. Mammals also have fur or hair to help them keep warm. Mammal mothers feed their babies milk from their body.

Three types of mammals

Mammals are divided into three groups—**monotremes**, **placentals**, and marsupials. Monotremes lay eggs from which their babies hatch.

Placentals and marsupials give birth to **live young**. Placental mammals grow inside their mother's body for at least a month. They receive food and **oxygen** through an organ called the **placenta**.

Growing in a pouch

A marsupial baby does not receive nutrients through a placenta as other mammals do. Most female marsupials have a pouch on their body. After the babies are born, they continue growing inside their mother's pouch.

Living on very little water

All living things need water to stay healthy. Animals drink water from rivers, lakes, or oceans in their **habitat**, or home. Most marsupials live in Australia, where the **climate** is mainly hot and dry. Little rain falls, and there are few lakes and rivers from which animals can drink. Australian animals have learned how to get moisture for their body in other ways. Some get water from the leaves or grasses they eat. Others are **nocturnal**, or active at night. They **conserve**, or hold, water in their body by searching for food at night, when the temperature is cooler.

(opposite page) The Virginia opossum is the only type of marsupial that lives in North America.

(below) This red kangaroo is drinking from a stream. Most of the time, however, kangaroos drink very little. They get the moisture their body needs from the grass they eat.

The marsupial family tree

There are over 250 **species**, or types, of marsupials. The largest species is the red kangaroo, which grows to be over six feet (2 m) tall and weighs 200 pounds (90 kg). The smallest species is the narrow-nosed planigale, which weighs only 0.2 ounces (6 g).

Male spotted cuscuses have spots, but females do not.

*A male red kangaroo is called a **boomer**. Females are called **blue fliers** because they have blue-gray fur.*

Plant-eating cousins

Even though these marsupials do not look alike, the species shown on this page are related. They are **herbivores**, or plant-eaters. Some, such as the koala and the wombat, are more closely related than others.

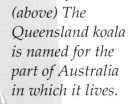

(above) The Queensland koala is named for the part of Australia in which it lives.

(left) Wombats are stout, short-legged marsupials.

Meat-eating marsupials

The marsupials shown here are **carnivores**, or meat-eaters. Some eat mainly insects, and others eat animals such as lizards, birds, and small kangaroos.

bilby

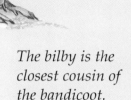

The bilby is the closest cousin of the bandicoot.

bandicoot

The marsupial mole is the only species in its group.

The narrow-nosed planigale is a type of marsupial mouse.

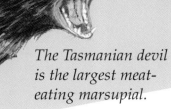

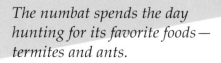

The Tasmanian devil is the largest meat-eating marsupial.

The numbat spends the day hunting for its favorite foods— termites and ants.

7

A marsupial's body

Marsupials come in many sizes and shapes. Their body is **adapted**, or suited, to the place where they live and the type of food they eat. Some marsupials are taller and heavier than an adult human, whereas others are small enough to fit in your hand. Some have a long tail for balance or gripping branches, but others have no tail at all. Most small marsupials have sharp, pointed teeth for tearing meat. Large marsupials that eat plants have flat, blunt teeth.

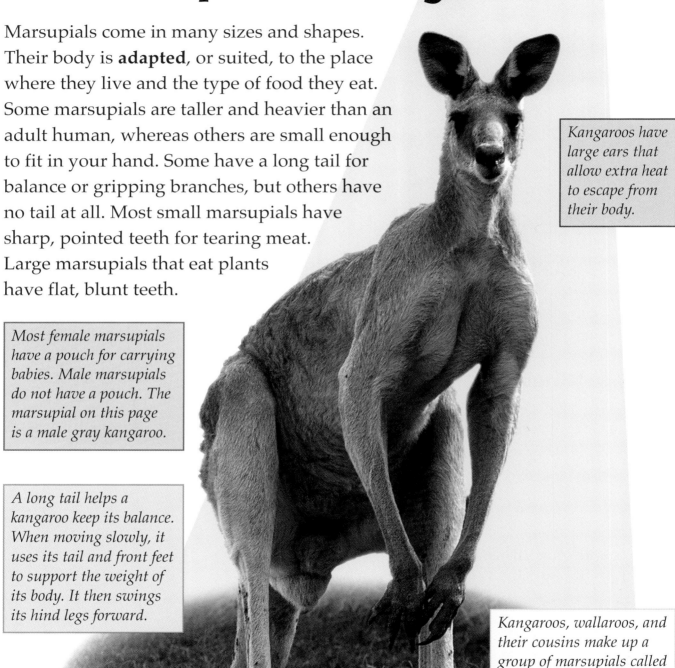

Kangaroos have large ears that allow extra heat to escape from their body.

Most female marsupials have a pouch for carrying babies. Male marsupials do not have a pouch. The marsupial on this page is a male gray kangaroo.

A long tail helps a kangaroo keep its balance. When moving slowly, it uses its tail and front feet to support the weight of its body. It then swings its hind legs forward.

Kangaroos, wallaroos, and their cousins make up a group of marsupials called **macropods**. Macropod means "big feet."

8

The nose knows

Bilbies and numbats find food by **rooting**, or digging with their long, pointed nose. They stick their snout into the soil and dead leaves on the ground and sniff out insects and insect **larvae** to eat.

bilby   *numbat*

To find juicy insect larvae, this antechinus uses its keen sense of smell when it roots through soil.

Built for climbing

The bodies of some marsupials are built for climbing. Opossums, shown right, have a **prehensile**, or grasping, tail. They use their long, strong tail as an extra limb to help them move around in the treetops.

Koalas do not have a tail. Instead, they move around in trees using their sharp claws, which dig into tree trunks. They have two **opposable** thumbs on each of their front paws and one thumb on each hind foot. Opposable thumbs allow some types of animals to grasp objects.

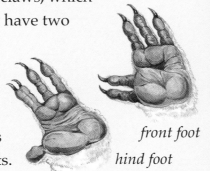

front foot

hind foot

9

In the pouch

(above) A female wombat's pouch faces the rear to prevent dirt from covering the baby inside while the mother is digging.

A mother marsupial's pouch provides her baby with warmth, protection, and a place to eat. Not all pouches are the same, however. Kangaroos and opossums have a pouch on their stomach that opens toward the front of the animal. Koalas, Tasmanian devils, and wombats have pouches that open toward the rear. Some marsupials do not have a pouch at all!

Bringing up baby

When a baby marsupial is born, it is tiny, blind, and its body is not fully developed. The baby must find its way from the birth opening into its mother's pouch. The baby pulls itself along its mother's body using only its front claws. Some marsupial mothers guide their baby by licking a path along their own belly.

When the baby reaches the pouch, it finds a nipple inside and begins **nursing**, or drinking milk. Some marsupials, such as opossums and marsupial mice, give birth to a **litter**, or group of babies. If the mother has more babies than nipples, some of the babies starve.

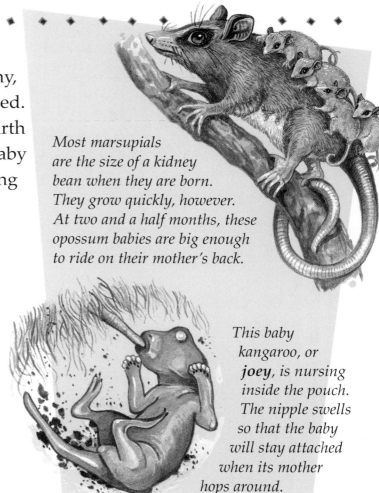

Most marsupials are the size of a kidney bean when they are born. They grow quickly, however. At two and a half months, these opossum babies are big enough to ride on their mother's back.

*This baby kangaroo, or **joey**, is nursing inside the pouch. The nipple swells so that the baby will stay attached when its mother hops around.*

Not all marsupials have a pouch!

Some marsupials have only a loose flap of skin on their belly that partly covers the baby's body. Others, such as this antechinus mouse, have no pouch at all. The mother gives birth to a large litter. The babies hang on to the mother's nipples for about five weeks. When they get too big and heavy, the mother builds a soft nest of grass, leaves, and flowers to keep the babies warm and protected while she hunts.

Kangaroos

Kangaroos are the best-known Australian animals. They live in Australia, Tasmania, and New Guinea. Red kangaroos, gray kangaroos, and wallaroos are the three largest species of macropods.

Chew on this!

Kangaroos are herbivores. They eat mainly grass, which is low in nutrients. To get as many nutrients as possible, kangaroos chew a **cud**. They chew a mouthful of grass, swallow it, and then bring it back up from their stomach and rechew the grass before swallowing it a second time.

Baby on board

Some parts of Australia have periods of **drought**, or low rainfall. Kangaroos can find little to eat or drink during a drought. Adult kangaroos usually drink very little, but a female carrying a baby needs water to keep her body healthy. If a joey cannot get enough nourishment from its mother, it could die.

After kangaroos **mate**, the female kangaroo stores a **fertilized** egg in her body. When there is enough food and water, the egg grows into a baby. After the baby is born, the female mates again and stores another egg. She keeps a fertilized egg in her body so that she will be ready to give birth when there is a good food supply.

(above) Kangaroos often rest in a shady spot during the hottest part of the day to help keep their body cool and save energy. A willie wagtail bird has found a safe perch on this lounging red kangaroo.

(left) Male kangaroos defend themselves against enemies by **boxing**, or punching and kicking. Males often fight over females. The largest male in a group will box with the other males to prove that he is the biggest and strongest.

'Roo cousins

Although the big kangaroos are the best known, there are more than 50 species of smaller kangaroos. Quokkas, wallabies, pademelons, bettongs, potoroos, woylies, and boodies are some types of small kangaroos.

Tree kangaroos

Tree kangaroos are **arboreal**, which means they live in trees. They have longer forelegs and shorter hind feet than kangaroos that live on the ground. When tree kangaroos build a nest, they use their tail to carry grass and branches. They cannot grasp tree branches with their tail, however. Rough pads on the soles of their feet help tree kangaroos grip tree trunks. Even though these marsupials are arboreal, they are not quick, agile climbers. They move slowly among the trees. During the day, most tree kangaroos sleep crouched up in the fork of a tree.

Tree kangaroos are the only kangaroos that are able to move their hind legs one at a time. They need to move one leg after the other in order to climb up and down trees.

Wallabies

Wallabies look very similar to red and gray kangaroos, but they are smaller than their cousins. Like bigger kangaroos, wallabies live in large groups called **mobs**.

Rat kangaroos

Rat kangaroos are named for their small size, which is about the same size as rats. They are also known as potoroos, which is an Aboriginal word meaning "long-nosed kangaroo."

(above) Rat kangaroos dig up insects and roots from thick scrubland areas.

(top) The feet of rock wallabies have rough soles to help them grip slippery rock surfaces.

Koalas

Many people think that koalas look like bears, but these marsupials are not bears! There are three types of koalas: the Victoria koala, the Queensland koala, and the New South Wales koala. All three types are arboreal. Koalas spend most of their time sleeping high above the ground in eucalyptus trees.

Leaf-eaters

Koalas are **folivores**, or leaf-eaters. Eucalyptus leaves are their favorite food. This type of food is low in nutrients, so koalas must eat many leaves in order to get the energy they need. Eucalyptus leaves also contain poisons, however. These poisons could harm other animals, but a koala's stomach can **digest**, or break down, the leaves to get the nutrients. The poisons are expelled from the koala's body.

Yawwwnnn...this koala is so sleepy! Koalas rest about twenty hours each day to save energy.

16

A close bond

Koalas are **solitary** animals. Male and female koalas spend little time together, but a mother koala spends up to one year with her baby, which is also called a joey. She carries her joey everywhere she goes. The mother carries her baby in her pouch and feeds it milk until it is six months old.

A taste of eucalyptus

At six months, the growing joey rides on its mother's back. The baby starts eating **pap**, which is a slimy green liquid made of digested eucalyptus leaves. Eating the pap helps the baby get used to the taste of eucalyptus. The baby feeds on its mother's milk and pap until it is a year old.

Wombats

Wombats are short, stocky marsupials that live in underground **burrows**, or holes. Burrows help wombats stay cool in summer and warm in winter.

Underground homes also provide safety. Wombats protect themselves from **predators** by blocking the entrance of the burrow with their behind. If a predator tries to enter the burrow, the wombat squeezes its enemy's head against the roof.

Wombats eat mainly tough, dry grass. They grind their food into tiny pieces to get more nutrients from it. A wombat's **incisors**, or front teeth, are designed to grow throughout its life so they will not wear out from constant grinding. Wombats are the only marsupials that have these teeth.

This wombat has a baby in her pouch. She squeezes muscles in her pouch to hold the baby in and relaxes them to let the baby climb out. Air circulates in the pouch so that the baby can breathe.

Wombat warrens

Several burrows are connected by tunnels to form a **warren**. Some wombat warrens are as long as 100 feet (30 m)! Up to ten wombats may live in a warren, but the animals spend little time together. They are very protective of their territory. If a male wombat comes into contact with another male, the two often fight!

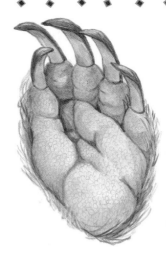

A wombat's paw is flat and wide with long, curved claws for digging.

A wombat's body is adapted to digging burrows. In addition to its strong front feet, the wombat has a broad head and shoulders for pushing dirt and widening the opening of its burrow.

Opossums

Possums and opossums are able to adapt to almost any habitat. Opossums live in North, South, and Central America. Possums live in Australia and New Guinea. Many of these marsupials live near people.

Playing dead

Have you ever heard the expression "playing possum?" When an opossum is scared, it lies very still and breathes slowly. This behavior fools its enemies into thinking the opossum is dead. If the opossum is lucky, the predator will lose interest and go away. Opossums can play dead for up to four hours.

Danger from people

Cars often hit and kill opossums. When a female opossum is hit by a car, she might die, but the babies in her pouch could survive. They will not live long, however, unless they are taken to an animal hospital where they can be treated.

Opossums spend most of their time in trees. They use their claws and tail to hang from branches and grab food that is out of reach.

This tiny pygmy possum often drinks nectar from flowers, but its favorite foods are insects and spiders.

20

Gliders

Gliders move from tree to tree by soaring through the air. To "fly," a glider jumps from a tree and stretches out its **patagia**, which are flaps of skin on either side of its body. The patagia create a wide kitelike surface. The glider floats easily, using its legs and tail to steer. It lands on all four feet.

Gliders are **omnivores**. They eat plants and animals including insects, flower nectar, and tree sap. To get at the sap, a glider scrapes away the bark with its sharp claws and waits for the thick sap to ooze out. Often the sap flows so slowly that the glider must wait until the next day to eat it!

Bandicoots

Bandicoots are small marsupials that live in the scrublands of Australia. Of all marsupials, bandicoots grow inside their mother's body for the shortest period of time. They grow for only 12 days before they move into her pouch.

Each bandicoot has its own **home range**, or area in which it hunts and builds its nest. Male bandicoots defend their home range from other males by biting, scratching, and kicking.

Most bandicoots are omnivorous. They eat insects, slugs, snails, earthworms, small lizards, and rodents as well as berries and plants. Some bandicoots, such as the Eastern barred bandicoot shown above, have a long snout that they use for finding food in soil and rotting wood. They dig holes with their sharp front claws and use their pointed nose to search out the insects and insect larvae that are inside.

The bilby

In Australia, the bilby is a favorite animal. Australians nicknamed the bilby "pinkie" because of its bright pink nose. Instead of the Easter bunny, Australian children are visited by the Easter bilby, which hides eggs and brings them small gifts! Few wild bilbies are left in Australia, however. Foxes and **feral** cats have killed many of them. The bilby must also compete with rabbits and livestock for food.

Like wombats, bilbies dig underground burrows. They have strong front legs and sharp claws for digging long, deep tunnels. Unlike wombats, however, bilbies do not share their home with other bilbies. The only time a bilby shares its burrow is during mating season, when a male and female live together for a short time. Afterwards, the female gives birth to a single baby, with which she shares her burrow.

The bilby uses its long tongue to lick insects, insect larvae, seeds, and fungi from the soil. It swallows large amounts of sand along with its food, so its droppings are made up mainly of sand!

The numbat

Numbats are the only marsupials that are truly **diurnal**, or active during the day. Most other marsupials rest or sleep during part of the day to avoid the heat of the sun. Numbats spend most of the day eating. At night, they sleep inside a hollow log in a nest made of leaves, shredded bark, and grass. These small marsupials hide in their nest to protect themselves from predators such as raptors.

The numbat's favorite foods are ants and termites. When it finds an anthill, a numbat scratches away the surface to expose the insects inside. It licks up its prey with its long, sticky tongue. Large **termitaries**, or termite homes, are too hard for the numbat to break into. Instead, it uses its tongue to search in the cracks on the surface of the termitary or waits for the insects to come out.

Numbats are easily recognized by their striped fur. They are also called "banded anteaters" because of their markings and eating habits.

Marsupial mice

Dunnarts, kowaris, kultarrs, ningauis, and antechinuses are all types of marsupial mice. They may look cute, but they are fierce predators! At night, they emerge from their hollow-log homes to hunt. They chase insects such as beetles, spiders, and cockroaches. Like larger predators, marsupial mice have sharp, pointed teeth for tearing meat. Scientists who study marsupial mice often receive painful bites on their fingers!

Short and sweet

Many marsupial mice have a very short life span. During mating season, male antechinuses stop feeding and spend all their time looking for a female mate. By the time the males have mated, their bodies are weak. They eventually die because their weak bodies cannot fight diseases and **parasites**. Most of the females are still healthy, however, and live long enough to have a second litter the following year.

(right) This antechinus mother builds a warm, dry nest for her young. She protects her babies from predators such as owls and snakes.

(above) Most marsupial mice are excellent hunters. They even attack insects their own size or larger! This planigale is sinking its teeth into a big, juicy grasshopper.

25

The Tasmanian devil

Tasmanian devils were named for their frightening appearance and piercing scream. These marsupials live in the rainforests of the island of Tasmania, which is part of Australia. Tasmanian devils are solitary animals. The only time several devils live together is when a female has a litter of babies. When the young devils are big enough to live outside their mother's pouch, their mother moves them into a nest of leaves and grasses.

When Tasmanian devils are excited, everyone else knows it! At first, they stamp their feet and show their sharp teeth. Their ears turn bright red, and they let out bloodcurdling screams. To make themselves look stronger and scarier, devils turn their body to the side and then quickly turn to face the enemy while baring their sharp teeth. They move so fast that they appear to be spinning around in circles. Most animals avoid fighting with a devil!

What's on the menu?

Tasmanian devils are not skilled hunters. Their hind legs are too weak to run fast enough to catch prey. Instead, devils wait for another animal to make a kill. When the hunter leaves, the devil feeds on the **carrion**, or animal carcass. The jaw of the Tasmanian devil is among the strongest in the animal kingdom. These marsupials can bite through almost anything—even thick wire. Tasmanian devils eat every part of their prey, including the bones.

Tasmanian devils eat a wide variety of foods including insects, fruit, garbage, eggs, small mammals, birds, and reptiles.

That's MY lunch!

Tasmanian devils fight for their meals. They shriek and snarl to scare away other animals, including devils. If these scare tactics do not work, the devils will attack. Their powerful jaws can cause painful wounds. Often one animal dies.

(right) This devil is eating a pademelon, which is a type of small kangaroo, but Tasmanian devils will even eat other devils!

27

Quolls

There are four species of quolls, or native cats: the eastern quoll, western quoll, northern quoll, and spotted-tail quoll. The first settlers who came to Australia named these marsupials "native cats" because they thought that quolls looked like house cats. Quolls spend most of their time on the ground, but the spotted-tail quoll has ridged pads on its feet so it can climb and hunt prey that lives in trees.

An unusual feature of quolls is their spotted fur. These markings provide **camouflage**. Most quolls are brown with white spots, but a few are black and white. The spotted-tail quoll is the only species that has spots on its tail.

The spotted-tail quoll, shown above, is the largest meat-eating marsupial on Australia's mainland. Quolls are agile hunters that prey on small birds, reptiles, mammals, and insects. They use their sharp teeth and claws to tear apart prey.

The marsupial mole

The marsupial mole is so different from other marsupials that scientists cannot agree on the group to which it belongs! Very little is known about the marsupial mole. It spends most of its life underground, digging through the loose sand of its desert habitat.

The marsupial mole has two flat claws on each of its front paws that it uses for burrowing. A hard plate on its nose protects its face as it digs. The marsupial mole is blind—it does not need good eyesight to live underground. It digs insect larvae out of the ground for food.

The marsupial mole's pouch opens to the rear to keep out sand while the animal digs. As the mole tunnels through the sand, the burrow collapses and fills in with sand. A marsupial mole's burrow is nearly impossible to see!

Marsupials in danger

As the population grows, people take over areas that were once home to wild animals. These kangaroos are sharing their grazing area with golfers.

Before European settlers arrived in Australia, most of the mammals that lived there were marsupials. Few animals preyed on them. When the settlers came, they brought new species of animals such as foxes, dogs, and cats with them. These animals began hunting marsupials. Many marsupial species were unable to defend themselves against these new predators and soon became **endangered** or **extinct**.

Move over marsupials

Kangaroos and livestock need large areas of land for grazing. Some farmers kill kangaroos so their herds of sheep and cattle will not have to compete with these marsupials for food. Today, laws protect kangaroos from hunters.

Gone forever

The largest marsupial carnivore was the thylacine, or Tasmanian wolf. Thylacines hunted mainly small kangaroos. When people began raising sheep in Australia, thylacines hunted the sheep as well. To protect their herds, shepherds killed thousands of thylacines. Scientists believe that many of these marsupials also became sick and died.

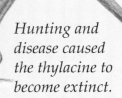

Hunting and disease caused the thylacine to become extinct.

30

Aboriginal patch-burning

Many years ago, the Aborigines of Australia hunted hare wallabies. They set fire to small patches of old dry grass so new grass would grow in its place. The Aborigines caught the wallabies at night when the animals came to eat the new grass. The Aborigines caught only the animals they needed.

In 1788, European settlers arrived in Australia, and the Aborigines were forced to change their way of life. They stopped patch-burning the land, and the grass grew tall and dry. Eventually, bush fires destroyed the grass. Many animals that lived in the grass, including wallabies, also died. Today, many of the Aborigines are again using the traditional method of patch-burning the land. As a result, some marsupial species are increasing in numbers.

Saving marsupial habitats

When people cut down trees for timber or take over land to make room for cities, marsupial homes are destroyed. Animals that cannot find food or shelter become endangered species. Wildlife organizations such as the Australian Koala Foundation work to preserve marsupial habitats and keep these animals safe.

*(right) Some marsupials such as this wombat live in **sanctuaries**, or parks in which animals and their habitats are protected.*

31

Words to know

Aborigine A native person of Australia
camouflage Colors or marks on an animal that help hide it from enemies
carrion Dead, rotted animal flesh
climate The weather that an area has had over a long period of time
endangered Describing an animal species that is in danger of dying out
extinct Describing a plant or animal that no longer exists
feral Describing an animal that was once tame but now lives and hunts in the wild
fertilized Describing an egg that is ready to grow into a baby
folivore An animal that eats mainly the leaves and stems of plants
larva The wormlike form of some insects

live young Describing a baby animal that is not hatched from an egg
mate (n) A partner for producing offspring ; (v) to reproduce, or make babies
oxygen A gas present in air that animals and plants need to breathe
parasite A creature that feeds off another animal's body
placenta The organ inside a pregnant mammal's body that provides food and air to the baby that is growing inside
placental Describing an animal that, before it is born, grows inside its mother's body along with the placenta
predator An animal that kills and eats prey
prey (n) An animal that is hunted and eaten by another animal; (v) to hunt an animal

Index

Aborigines 15, 31
Australia 5, 6, 12, 20, 22, 23, 26, 28, 30, 31
babies 4, 8, 10-11, 12, 17, 18, 20, 23, 25, 26
bandicoots 7, 22
bilbies 7, 9, 23
bodies 4, 5, 6, 8-9, 11, 13, 16, 19, 21, 22, 23, 25, 26
burrows 18, 19, 23, 29
cuscuses 6
dangers 20, 30-31
enemies *see predators*

food 4, 5, 6, 7, 8, 9, 10, 12, 16, 17, 18, 20, 21, 22, 23, 24, 26, 27, 28, 29, 30, 31
fur 4, 6
homes 5, 8, 29, 30, 31
insects 7, 9, 15, 20, 21, 22, 23, 24, 25, 27, 28, 29
joeys 11, 12, 17
kangaroos 5, 6, 7, 8, 10, 11, 12-15, 27, 30
koalas 6, 9, 10, 16-17, 31
marsupial mice 7, 9, 11, 25
marsupial moles 7 , 29

nests 11, 14, 22, 24, 25, 26
numbats 7, 9, 24
opossums 5, 9, 10, 11, 20
pouches 4, 8, 10-11, 17, 22, 26, 29
predators 18, 20, 23, 24, 25, 30
rat kangaroos 15
tails 8, 9, 14, 20, 21
Tasmanian devils 7, 10, 26-27
tree kangaroos 14
wallabies 14, 15, 31
wallaroos 8, 12
water 5, 12
wombats 6, 10, 18, 23, 31

1 2 3 4 5 6 7 8 9 0   Printed in the U.S.A.   9 8 7 6 5 4 3 2 1 0